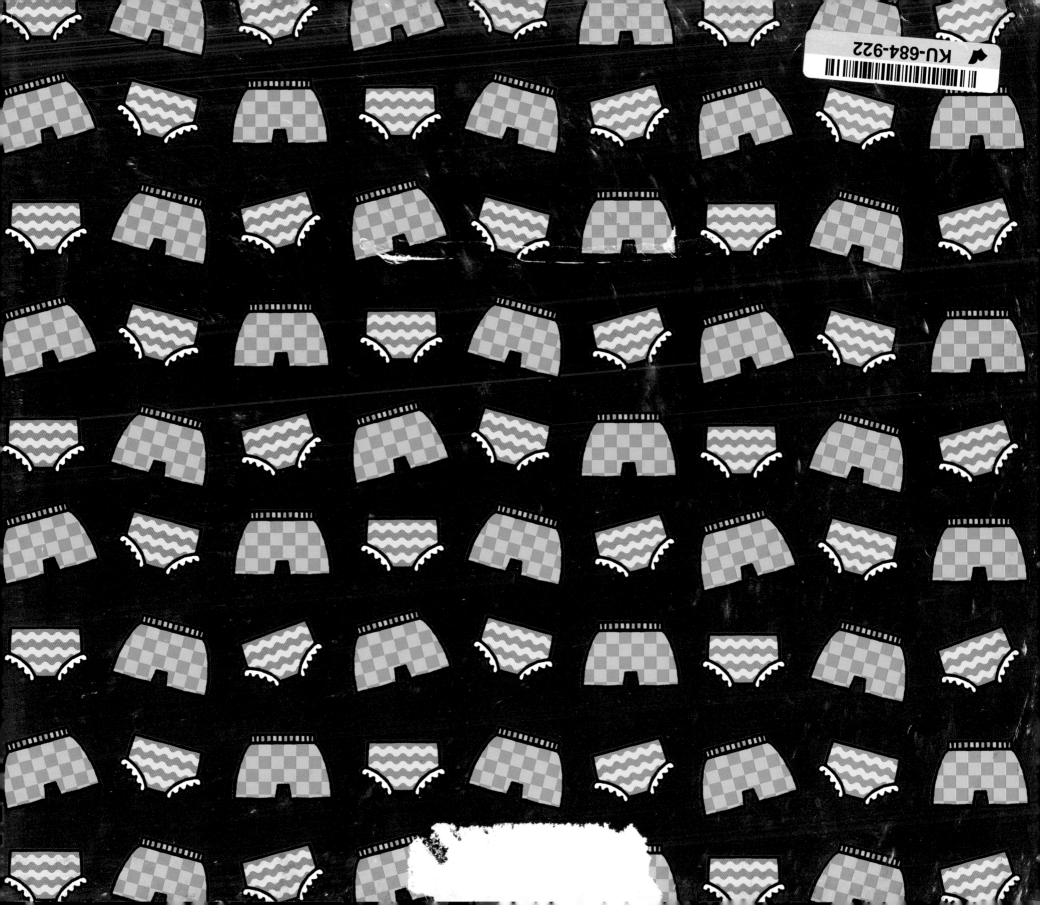

For Jackson – G.A.
For Pam, John, Maya and Sienna – N.S.

MORE PANTS
A DAVID FICKLING BOOK 978 0 385 61077 3

Published in Great Britain by David Fickling Books,
a division of Random House Children's Books

This edition published 2007

1 3 5 7 9 10 8 6 4 2

Text copyright © Giles Andreae, 2007
Illustrations copyright © Nick Sharratt, 2007

DAVID FICKLING BOOKS
31 Beaumont Street, Oxford, OX1 2NP
a division of RANDOM HOUSE CHILDREN'S BOOKS
61–63 Uxbridge Road, London W5 5SA
A division of The Random House Group Ltd

RANDOM HOUSE AUSTRALIA (PTY) LTD
20 Alfred Street, Milsons Point, Sydney,
New South Wales 2061, Australia

RANDOM HOUSE NEW ZEALAND LTD
18 Poland Road, Glenfield, Auckland 10, New Zealand

RANDOM HOUSE (PTY) LTD
Isle of Houghton, Corner Boundary Road & Carse O'Gowrie,
Houghton 2198, South Africa

RANDOM HOUSE INDIA PVT LTD
301 World Trade Tower, Hotel Intercontinental Grand Complex,
Barakhamba Lane, New Delhi 110001, India

THE RANDOM HOUSE GROUP Limited Reg. No. 954009
www.kidsatrandomhouse.co.uk

A CIP catalogue record for this book is available from the British Library.

Printed in China

More Pants

Giles Andreae

Nick Sharratt

David Fickling Books

OXFORD · NEW YORK

Red pants, green pants

Yellow submarine pants

Tickling your tummy pants

And matching bra!

Never getting wetty pants

Supersonic jetty pants

Arty pants,
party pants

Black belt in karate pants

Have you done a farty pants?

Puffy pants, fluffy pants

Pants
for a
scary
dinosaur

hotter pants

Aren't there
such a lotta pants?

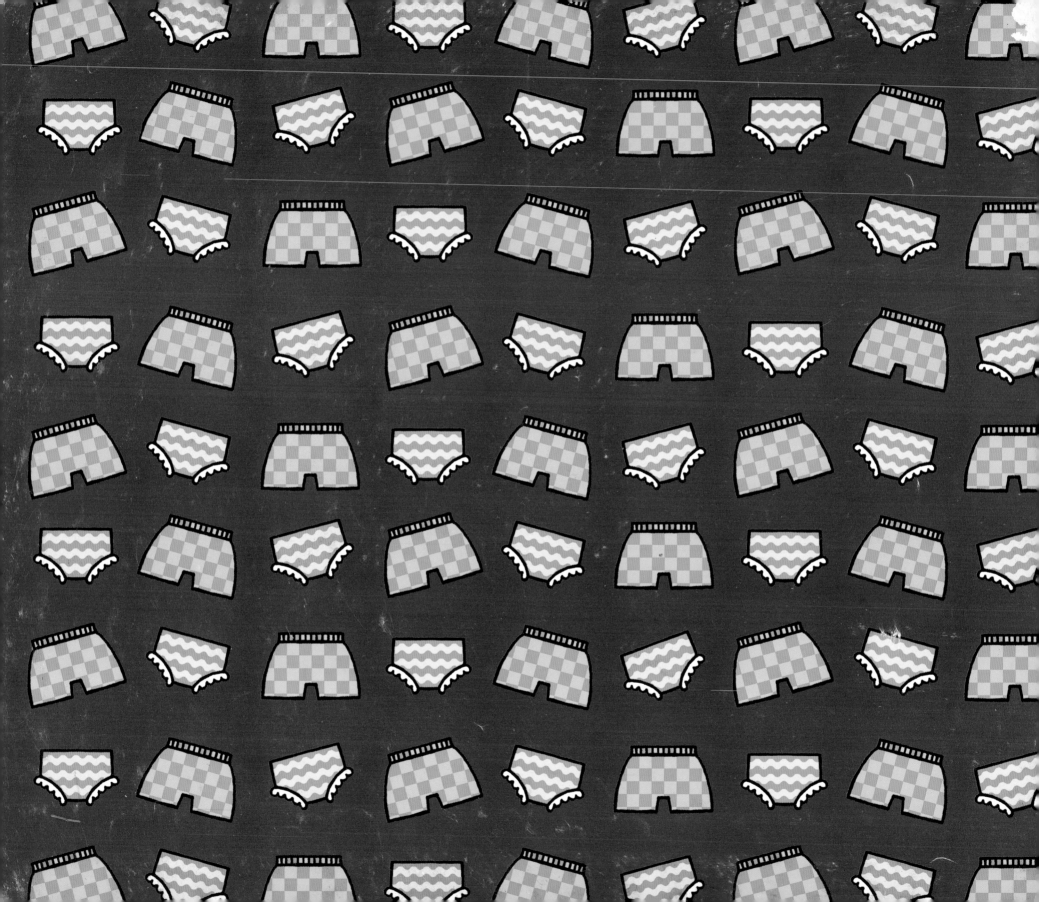